IMAGES OF ENGLAND

BRIXHAM
REVISITED

IMAGES OF ENGLAND

BRIXHAM
REVISITED

TED GOSLING

The
History
Press

Frontispiece: A summer afternoon in June 1984, with holidaymakers enjoying the sun beside the William of Orange statue on the waterfront. (Courtesy of the *Express and Echo*)

First published in 2005 by Tempus Publishing

Reprinted in 2010 by
The History Press
The Mill, Brimscombe Port,
Stroud, Gloucestershire, GL5 2QG
www.thehistorypress.co.uk

British Library Cataloguing in Publication Data.
A catalogue record for this book is available from the British Library.

ISBN 978 0 7524 3620 3

Typesetting and origination by Tempus Publishing.
Printed and bound in England by
Marston Book Services Limited, Oxford

Contents

Acknowledgements

My thanks must go to those wonderful Brixham people who gave time to talk about their native town, contributing valuable information in the compilation of this book.

I am most grateful for the kindness and help given to me by David James, all pictures in this book (unless otherwise stated) come from his wonderful collections of bygone Brixham.

My thanks must go again to Ken Thomas, Maurice Snell, Ralph Gardner, Alf Worth, Mrs M. Pack and the *Express and Echo* for the pictures which I used in a previous book, and used again in this publication. Thanks must go to Norman Lambert for his introduction, and to Mrs Lyn Marshall for her help. The accuracy of the facts in this book have been checked as carefully as possible. However, original sources can contain errors, and memories fade over the years. The dates presented are often opinions, and when accompanied by a '*c.*' may be ten years out.

Old photographs are truly fascinating. They bring back so vividly times past, and to live in them is never to die. To the young, the past must seem like a foreign land, but the generation born before the Second World War recognize its beauty and are left with a haunting sense of loss.

Ted Gosling
May 2005

Introduction

Much has already been written and recorded by pictures of this attractive fishing port, tucked into Torbay in the south coast of Devon.

That said, in this age of modern technology where the old-fashioned photograph and postcard of a century ago are becoming increasingly rare, it is both exciting and interesting to have a further pictorial record captured with pictures from the past. In this latest book, Ted Gosling has produced another fine collection of old Brixham photographs, with the help of one of the town's major collectors, David James, who is a native of Brixham and who works in the fish market. David has a wealth of knowledge about happenings both past and present, and has built up a substantial collection of local illustrated material, which he has accumulated with great enthusiasm and care over many years.

If only some of the characters who appear in the photographs could come back to see Brixham as it is today, and tell their stories of yesteryear. With modern methods of communication, one could envisage long queues of interested parties stretching from East Devon in one direction to Plymouth in the other, to listen to the interest this picturesque port has generated.

May Devonians, especially the people of Brixham, together with the many visitors it attracts, enjoy Ted's latest book, and may it remain a sought-after and lasting addition to the Brixham archives in the years ahead.

Norman Lambert
May 2005

The fish market, Brixham, *c.* 1920.

British Legion Knitting Circle, Brixham, February 1940.

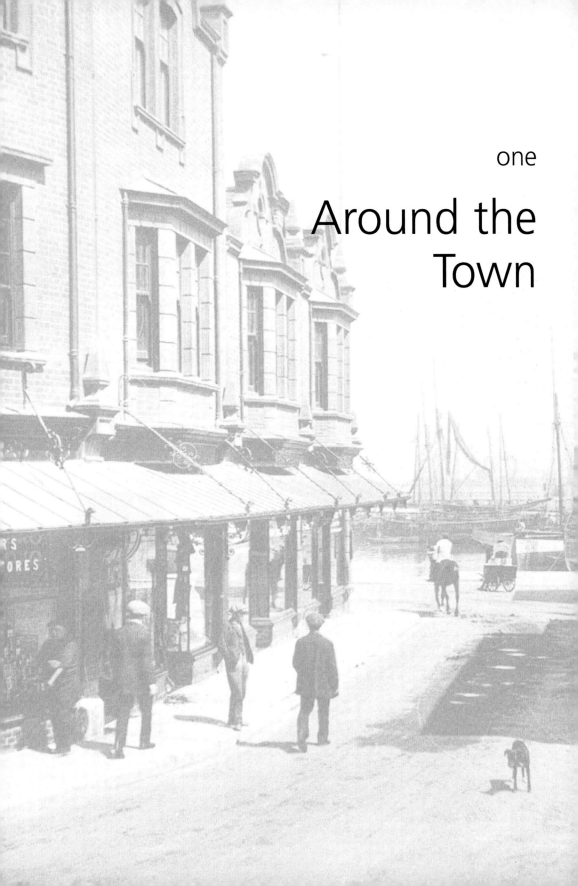

one

Around the Town

Fore Street & Strand, Brixham.

Above: Fore Street and Strand, *c.* 1912.

Left: Fishermen standing on Broad Steps, Brixham, 1905. Broad Steps was once the home of the Dalton family.

Fore Street, Brixham, c. 1925. The Brixham Co-operative Society shop on the left was then managed by Mr W.J. Shutte. You can see by the horse-drawn vehicle that they were still using this form of transport for deliveries. Further back on the right you can pick out Jabez Doidge's Temperance Hotel at No. 52.

The Cottage Hospital, Brixham, c. 1903. The old Cottage Hospital in Cavern Road was opened in 1895 at a cost of £1,500, a sum funded by Miss A.M. Hogg.

Fore Street, Brixham.

Above: Peter Williams' Fancy Repository, No. 39 Fore Street, Brixham, *c.* 1919. Despite the name, this was only a shop, but you could get anything there and enjoy service that would not be thought possible today. The man in the doorway on the right was Mr Bicknell, who kept a confectioner's and paper shop. Union Lane, opposite, was generally known as 'Foxes Lane', because Fox & Co. had a grocer's shop at No. 26, at the top of the lane.

Left: The 83 Steps, *c.* 1910. These steps connected Higher Street to Prospect Road, and climbing up and down four times a day kept Brixham residents at the peak of health.

Rockberry Restaurant near Berry Head, with Round Top in the background, *c.* 1930.

The Northcliffe Hotel, pictured here in 1953, was built after the First World War and was for many years the social meeting place for the town. The hotel was demolished in 1996 following an earlier fire which had destroyed the building.

The Prince of Orange Statue on Brixham Quay, *c.* 1914. On 5 November 1688 William, Prince of Orange landed at Brixham at the invitation of the Whig leaders. The statue, mounted on a 10ft-high granite pedestal, depicts William with his right foot on a rock, his right hand holding his hat, with his left hand on his heart.

Above: A summer afternoon in Brixham, August 1910. The photographer had stopped in Berry Head Road to capture this peaceful scene of the Edwardian Brixham Harbour.

Right: The Coffin House, Brixham, *c.* 1908. Said to be 600 years old, this much–photographed building was occupied by a barber's shop in 1908. The sign on the wall states, 'Ye Olde Coffin House, Only One In England'.

Old Coffin House, Brixham

Queens Road, Brixham, taken before the First World War. Here, on a sunny day nearly a century ago, the absence of motor traffic in Queens Road does tend to prove one of the disadvantages of the motor car. The road was still free from petrol fumes and was still a place of peace and quiet in the early twentieth century.

A fine architectural picture of Brixham Baptist Chapel, *c.* 1910. This Baptist Chapel in Market Street was first founded in 1797, was rebuilt in 1858 and restored in 1895.

Before the Second World War people on holiday were eager to have a keepsake to remind them of their stay in Brixham. Holiday makers often paid a visit to Smardons Library and Stationery shop at Bolton Cross. The shop belonged to H.M. 'Spot' Smardon, a man who was involved in many of the organisations of the town, and who dedicated his life to the service of the Brixham community.

Before the Second World War the townspeople always celebrated Empire Day, and flags were hung from first-floor windows along the streets. It was held on Queen Victoria's birthday, 24 May, and originated as a commemoration of the assistance given by the colonies in the Boer War 1899-1902. In this picture we have Jones' Corner Dairy – King Street and Fore Street – decorated with flags and bunting for Empire Day, 1932.

The Town Chute, *c.* 1910. The Town Chute stood in St Mary's Square and supplied water in the days when the majority of people in Higher Brixham did not have a water main to their homes. The Town Chute was demolished in the 1930s and a public telephone box was then erected on the site.

Annie Tolcher's Cottage, Milton Street, Higher Brixham.

Annie Tolcher's Cottage, Milton Street, Higher Brixham, 1904.

The chimneys of the old Devonshire houses are very distinctive, as illustrated by these houses in Higher Brixham. These houses were demolished in the 1920s.

Summer Lane, Higher Brixham, *c.* 1900. 'Up Cowtown' was the name given by the fishermen of Lower Brixham to Higher Brixham, when the area was mainly a farming community.

Left: Higher Street, with the steps to Overgang in the background.

Below: The Old Homestead, Greenover Farm, Brixham, 1900. Farm houses like this are complementary to the English landscape, and were formerly the habitations of yeomen who farmed and worked on the land. These people, like their fathers before them, lived in direct contact with the soil, and the land was their great benefactor. In recent years retired people and refugees from urban life are buying up old farm houses, and new money, together with metropolitan attitudes, is transforming them.

The road to Berry Head, taken in 1905. The houses on the right were then occupied by the local coastguards.

The Town Hall at Bolton Cross, New Road, 1903. This building stands on the old site of a reservoir, built in around 1700 to supply fresh water to naval shipping. At a later date this water was piped to King's Quay at the entrance to the Inner Harbour.

This fine aerial view was taken from the top of St Mary's church tower, *c.* 1958.

Parkham Towers Hotel, Brixham, *c.* 1936.

The Commercial Inn, next to the Crown and Anchor, which can be seen on the left, *c.* 1935.

BRIXHAM.

This superb historic photograph of Brixham was taken around 1932 and you can see that the guns were still in place beside the statue to William, Duke of Orange. Pictures like this provide a lasting record of Brixham's houses and public buildings, shops, businesses and pubs, some are unchanged, while others have vanished or been altered almost beyond recognition.

Opposite, above: Overgang Steps, *c.* 1908. This evocative picture of Overgang Steps, taken early in the twentieth century, came from a postcard.

Opposite, below: Bolton Cross and Town Hall, *c.* 1908. The Town Hall and market were built on a site presented to Brixham by W.H. Nelson Esq. The police station next to the Town Hall was built in 1902 and is now the home of the museum. The sergeant in charge in those days was Richard Moon, who had five constables under his command.

Bolton Cross & Town Hall,
Brixham.

The eastern end of Fore Street, *c.* 1898. Stone's shop, in the centre, stood on an area known as 'The Island', which was demolished in 1908 during road widening. Lloyds Bank now stands on the site, at the corner of Pump Street.

Opposite, above: Burton Corner Stores (W.G. Sweet). This was the former site of the Freemason's Lodge, and stood at the corner of Burton Street and Bolton Street. The Burton bus on the right in this picture was used on local services.

Opposite, below: A view of the British Seaman's Orphan Boys' Home from Rock House, *c.* 1935.

The Home from Rock House.
British Seamen's Orphan Boys Home. Brixham.

MODERN JOINERY CONTRACTOR

The Electrical Joinery Works

Bolton Street - Brixham

F. POTTER. Proprietor

ENQUIRIES INVITED

TELEPHONE 62

Left: An advertisement for the Electrical Joinery Works in Bolton Street, *c.* 1930.

Below: The camping site at the Brixham Holiday Camp, *c.* 1938.

Overgang House, *c.* 1948.

Berry Head House Hotel.

Above and below: Berry Head House Hotel was built as a military hospital during the Napoleonic Wars (1807–09), and in 1823 Revd Henry Francis Lyte, the author of the hymn 'Abide with me', took up residence there. In the top picture we have a view of Berry Head House as a hotel, around 1947, and in the bottom picture a postcard commemorating Revd Henry Francis Lyte.

BRIXHAM

The Rev.
HENRY FRANCIS LYTE
First Vicar of All Saints'
(Lower Brixham) 1824-1847
Author of "Abide with me"

*The original Church of All Saints'
(Lower Brixham) 1824*

Abide with me; fast falls the eventide;
The darkness deepens; Lord, with me abide;
When other helpers fail, and comforts flee,
Help of the helpless, O abide with me.

*All Saints' (Lower Brixham) 1947
Henry Lyte Memorial Church*

THE BRIXHAM CAVERN NO. 8A

Above and right: In 1858, during the progress of quarrying, a cavern containing stalactites and bones was discovered, and thoroughly explored by the Royal Geological Society. The depth of the cavern exceeds 600ft and the stalactites were known for the character of their formation. More than 1,800 different specimens were also recovered, consisting of flint implements, bones and teeth. In the top picture are some of the remarkable stalactites and in the right-hand picture the entrance to the caves – at one time the cavern was open to the public.

OPEN DAILY DURING THE SEASON

COME TO THE BRIXHAM CAVERN

CAVERN ENTRANCE

THE BRIXHAM CAVERN

Statue to William, Duke of Orange, Southern Quay, Brixham, *c.* 1936. William, Duke of Orange, who became King William III, landed in Brixham on 5 November 1688 for the Protestant revolution that ended the Stuart dynasty. A stone, which first commemorated his landing, became the landing stone for the Duke of Clarence, later William IV, who visited Brixham as the Lord High Admiral in 1823. Half of this stone now forms a tablet at the pier end, which was inscribed in commemoration of his visit, 23 July 1823.

Opposite, above: The Marine Walk, Brixham, *c.* 1950.

Opposite, below: Demolition of Lakemans Brewery, *c.* 1950. The Brewery stood at the rear of Fore Street. On the left-hand side of this picture you can see the Baptist church school room, with Brewery Lane on the right.

MARINE WALK, BRIXHAM. 25605

Brixham Pier.

Above: The Inner and Outer Harbour, *c.* 1910. The tall chimney in the background belongs to the Pure Ice Co.

Left: These people were visiting Brixham in June 1936. The photograph was taken on the Middle Pier, with Bigwood's ice factory in the background.

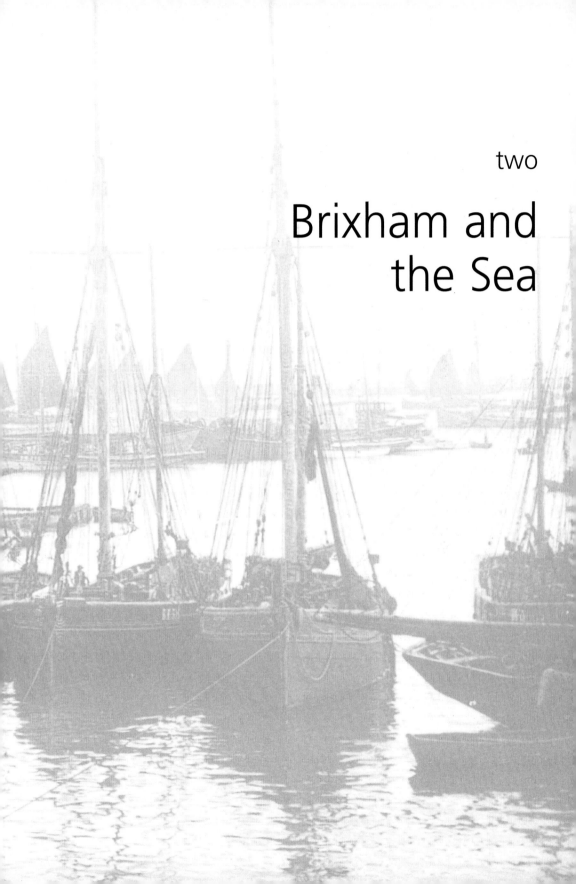

two

Brixham and
the Sea

Above and below: Brixham suffered a severe storm on the night of 10 January 1866, when more than forty ships anchored in Torbay were wrecked. The storm started out SSW force 10, then it veered NE force 11 to hurricane force 12. A monument was erected, to the memory of those who died, by the Brixham Shipwrecked Sailors Relief Committee, from the surplus of another relief fund. In the bottom picture are wrecks at Brixham, taken on 11 January 1866 following the storm, and above is all that remains of wooden sailing vessels wrecked against the harbour wall the same day.

BRIXHAM 1868

Above: Old photographs gain a special value, and this one of the fishing fleet at Brixham in 1868 is among the earliest of the town.

Below: Preparing the fish at Brixham, *c.* 1912. Then, as today, the sight, the sound and the smell of the sea are everywhere in the town, and this visually valuable photograph shows an everyday working practice of that time.

BRIXHAM FROM PROSPECT ROAD.

The whole economy of Brixham was based on fishing, shipbuilding and supporting trades. In the 1840s there were 270 sailing vessels in the port and by the beginning of the twentieth century the number stood at just over 200. In this fine photograph, taken on 9 August 1912, wooden sailing vessels lie against the harbour wall, with the dark sails of the fishing fleet can be seen beyond.

Opposite, above: If there was ever a competition to see who in this country worked hardest under the greatest discomfort, the fishermen from Brixham would have come high on the list. Smacks from the fishing fleet can be seen here in the Inner Harbour at the beginning of the twentieth century. At that time, Brixham had earned the proud title 'mother of the deep-sea fisheries'.

Opposite, below: The Inner and Outer Harbour, *c.* 1920. The chimney of the Brixham Ice Co. can be seen to the right in the picture.

The Fish Market, Brixham.

The fish market, Brixham, *c.* 1922.

Opposite, above: A delightful picture of Brixham trawlers, with a pleasure steamer from Torquay arriving in the harbour. Once a familiar sight in Brixham, the man in the rowing boat in the foreground is single-oar sculling. The rowing boat had no rowlocks, and the oar fitted in the half-moon shape in the stern. These boats were kept upside down on the foredeck of the trawlers.

Opposite, below: The fish market, *c.* 1921.

Brixham Harbour, *c.* 1910. In 1910 there were 213 trawlers, of various sizes and types, fishing off Brixham, and nine out of ten of the young men of the town went to sea.

Opposite, above: BM 125, *Winnie*, seen here in 1925, was owned by Jack Crocker. The Brixham trawlers were developed in Brixham in the late eighteenth century, and were one of the most powerful types of sailing vessels, for their size, ever built. Today only a few of these 75ft vessels remain, now used as yachts.

Opposite, below: The Inner Harbour, around 1909, with Peter Munday's shipyard in the background. The special quality of Brixham's past is reflected in this photograph. At that time there were 213 trawlers fishing from the port and the Brixham fishing fleet returning in the evening under full sail must have been a breathtaking sight.

54039 Brixham.

The Fish Market   Brixham

Accurate exposure has captured the afternoon sunshine in this 1928 photograph of Brixham Harbour. By this time, the famous Brixham fishing fleet was down to less than fifty vessels. Fish prices were falling, and by 1935 only twenty-six boats were left on the register, and some of these were even being sold for conversion into private yachts.

Opposite, above: A fine Edwardian picture of the fish market, 1909. The average weekly catch was about 150 tons, but sometimes as much as 350 tons were sold on the Quay in a week.

Opposite, below: Although Brixham men fished all round England, and were well known for finding new grounds, by 1934, when this picture of the Timer Harbour was taken, the trawling fleet at Brixham was in steady decline. However, in the 1970s and '80s there was a revival in the fortunes of the fishing fleet, although by this time the boats were equipped with all the latest aids.

Tales of the hardship involved in wresting a living from the sea are general, and many were told on return to the old fish market, pictured here during the 1920s.

Opposite, above and below: Although Brixham held its position as the leading fishing port in the country, until recent times an old saying in Beer went, 'Beer made Brixham and Brixham made the North Sea'. This was quite true, as the first fishermen to trawl from Brixham were men of Beer in their small boats. The best weather for trawling was a stiff breeze of not less than force 6, but this made the old Beer luggers weather-bound on the beach, because Beer did not have a harbour. As a result, Brixham, with its harbour, became the trawling centre. Despite this, Beer is still a fishing village, and the fishermen of Beer, like the men in these pictures, fully deserve their reputation of unsurpassed seamanship. The top picture shows a three-mast fishing lugger on Beer Beach in August 1877 and the bottom, Beer fishermen, *c.* 1960. (Courtesy of Seaton Museum)

FISHMARKET BRIXHAM.

This relaxed, uncrowded scene at Brixham was taken in the 1930s.

Opposite, above: Brixham Inner Harbour, *c.* 1958. Brixham is still a fishing port, although its glory has departed, and no longer can we see the brown sails of the famous Brixham trawlers. Until the Second World War there were still a few relying on sails, but by the time of this picture the internal combustion engine was used on all the boats, and the port has lost some of its picturesque appearance.

Opposite, below: The fish market, Brixham, *c.* 1930. Once the catch was brought ashore it was soon sold. The auction would begin early in the morning and last until midday. In the 1930s, the fisheries were in decline, and the fleet had fallen to less than thirty vessels.

The *Sunlit Waters*, a trawler from Lowestoft, lays up against the harbour wall, *c.* 1946. This was a time when much of the old Devonshire character could still be found in Brixham, especially by the quayside. Here most of the activity of men and ships was engaged in the work of the fishing industry rather than the entertainment of tourists and visitors.

Opposite, above: Brixham Harbour, *c.* 1925. Trawlers in the Inner Harbour, the fish market on the quay and the tiers of fishermen's homes in the background all combine to make this a typical photograph of the town in the 1920s.

Opposite, below: Seagulls are a feature of any seaside town, and the herring gulls seen here in Brixham Harbour, around 1960, have the ability to eat almost anything, making them one of the most successful species in Britain and perhaps the commonest of our gulls.

The Harbour, Brixham   9805

Brixham Harbour, 29 August 1939. A peaceful scene in late August, but within a few days it would all change. The time of appeasement would end at eleven o'clock on 3 September when Mr Chamberlain, speaking in a strained voice on the radio, informed the nation that we were at war with Germany.

Brixham Quay, 1938.

HMS *Brixham*, 1941. HMS *Brixham* was part of the Royal Navy's minesweeping flotilla, serving in the Mediterranean in the Second World War.

HMS *Mediator*, B Class tug, Brixham, 1949.

The screech of seagulls and the smell of salt air play an integral part of any fish market. In this picture, taken in the 1960s before the new fish market, the days catch is being sorted and graded ready for auction at the quayside market.

A busy quayside scene at Brixham fish market, *c.* 1963. Note the aluminium barrels, which replaced the old wooden barrels, for keeping the fish.

The Harbour, Brixham, 1951.

The Inner Harbour at Brixham, *c.* 1933. It was still an active fishing port, though the number of boats engaged in full-time fishing had sadly diminished.

Although by 1939 only half a dozen boats of Brixham's once proud fishing fleet were left, a revival came in the 1960s and later a new fish market and deep water jetty, with its own ice-making plant, was opened in 1971. This picture, taken in the 1960s, shows the harbour packed with trawlers. (Courtesy of the *Express and Echo*)

three

The People

The men who worked in Jackman's Yard, the shipbuilders, *c.* 1911. From left to right, back row: Harry Bond, Bill Moore, George Bond, Bill Salisbury, Robert Jackman, Harry Preston, Ralph Clark, Cyril Carey. Middle row: Harry Sherrif, Frank Lane, Mr Coyde, Billy Jackman, Tom Jackman, Jack Butler, Frank Hockley, Charlie Butle. Front row: Tom Stockman, Em Jackman, -?-, Mr Allery. Jack Butler, seen here with all the youth and vigour of a young man, lived to be 102 and died in 1993. (Courtesy of Alf Worth)

Brixham trawler men at the fish market, *c.* 1930. For these men fishing meant long hours and hard work, coupled with the fact that a good catch did not necessarily mean a good profit. The group includes Mr Allen and Lawyer Barnes.

Nets were braided by hand, and in this posed photograph, from around 1925, we see Mr Matthews braiding a fishing net at Mill Tye.

Jackman's Yard was beside Break Water Beach. It was one of the five busy shipbuilding yards where the sailing trawlers of Brixham were built. Here, in 1934, some of Jackman's skilled workforce stop work for this picture to be taken.

Above: Until recent years boats were built and repaired within the communities that used them, and the skills of men like these from Upham's Yard were always in demand. Sadly all this has now changed, but the men who worked in the Brixham shipyards are still remembered by all those who still go down to the sea to fish.

Right: Fishermen's wives gather in Higher Street, *c.* 1910.

Above: The Brixham British Legion Band, *c.* 1927. This band were formerly known as The Excelsior Band, Brixham.

Left: These four ladies with such happy smiles worked in the Torbay Paint Co. in New Road, Brixham. Although the picture can be dated to some time in the 1930s, no other details of this photograph are known.

Opposite, below: Pictured here in 1948 are the lady factory staff. From left to right, back row: Violet Tribble, Sylvia Harris, Miss Lynn, Eileen May, Hazel Snell. Middle row: Joyce Stapleton, Miss Putt, Loveday Tribble, Blanche Woolland, May George, Lena Weymouth. Front row: -?-, Miss Vigeon, Hefty Harris, Miss Tribble, Dolly Wright, -?-. (Courtesy of M. Pack)

The Torbay Paint Co. started in 1840 with works below Black Ball on the approach to the Freshwater Quarry, using the local red oxide ore. The paint works moved to New Road, Brixham before the Second World War, where they made camouflage paint.

The Torbay Paint Co. was bought out by Courtaulds, who decided it was too small to operate and closed the works in the late 1960s. This was rather a sad end to a successful local company that had operated for over 120 years. Pictured here in 1948 are the male staff members. From left to right, back row: –?–, Jack Harris, Harold Harvey, Frank Ash, Charlie Blackmore, Henry Poole. Second row: Em Mitchell, Arthur Whitten, John Avery, Bob Storey, Peter Collier, Joe Tribble, Henry German, Bruce Stutteridge, 'Felix'. Third row: Jim Eatock, Randall Harris, Jim Davey, George Boon, Bill Pocock. Front row: Ernie Higgs, Ken Sloman, Ken Marshall, young Joe Tribble, Mr Harvey. (Courtesy of M. Pack)

Brixham Swimming Club, 1977. From left to right, back row: Kevin Dart, Andrew Young, John Alberici, Paul Alberici, Linda Criddle, Janet Clark. Front row: Nicola Thomas, Sally Alberici, Karen Thomas, Mrs Irene Bradfield (coach), Julie Pope, Rachel Munnings, Andrew Heard. (Courtesy of Ken Thomas)

Opposite, above: Brixham National School, *c.* 1908.

Opposite, below: Taking a group picture of schoolboys is not easy. Persuading them to look at you, look cheerful and keep their eyes open can present problems. In this picture of pupils from the Furzeham Boys' School, taken around 1947, you can see by the end result that the photographer's succeeded in his task.

Above: Furzeham School, *c.* 1951. A mixed primary school, with boys' secondary school. James Callaghan, the former Labour Prime Minister, who died in March 2005, attended this school.

Left: Young David James looks somewhat uncertain about the parrot perched on his shoulder, although he appears to be coping well with the one that he is holding. It was 1961 and young David is pictured here with his sister Megan at a fairground in Brixham.

Opposite, below: A well-known character who set up his easel on the Quay was Laurie George, the artist known to everybody as Hippo. He can be seen here during the 1960s, busy completing a picture of the harbour, with a young admirer ready to help him.

Taken in 1940, this photograph of Brixham Spurs AFC is typical of its time and kind. The Spurs were winners of the Junior Cup during the 1939/40 season, and the pride of this achievement is reflected in their faces. (Courtesy of the E.S. Gosling collection)

Above: Annie Seaward is pictured here outside her shop on the Quay, *c.* 1930. She was licensed to sell tobacco, but also supplied crab teas. Crab sandwiches with your afternoon tea certainly sounds much more appetising than the Devon cream tea, and Grannie Seaward, as she was known locally, could probably put on a good Brixham spread.

Left: The ladies with walking sticks are seen here on Brixham Quay and the fish market in the background. This picture was taken in the 1930s, an era which opened in depression and ended in war, and, by the way they are dressed, these ladies appear to be middle-class visitors.

Right: The wedding of Frank Coleman and Jessie Snell, *c.* 1936. Unfortunately, Frank was one of the first Brixham casualties of the Second World War. He worked on one of the boats commandeered for naval use. It was blown up by a sea mine. (Courtesy of M. Snell)

Below: Pictured here are two members of the Brixham lifeboat crew in 1926, Bill Mugridge left, and Bill Pillar.

Above: The colourful scene of local fishermen on Brixham Quay, offering mackerel fishing, conger fishing and River Dart trips, was a regular feature of Brixham. This photograph, with mackerel fishing at 5s a head, is from the 1960s.

Left: For the past 400 years the life of Brixham was in fishing, boat building and all the subsidiary trades. Before the Second World War the five ship yards were always kept busy. The three men who posed for this photograph during the 1930s were a part of this world, and worked as boilermakers for Jackman's Yard.

Opposite, below: Brixham Furzehill Bowling Club proudly posing with their shield. Those present included Bryan Counter, Cyril Lawrence, John Skedgell, Harry Hamling, Will Smith, Mrs Minnie Hatherley, Cyril Burrow, Toots Skedgell, Mrs Mabel Hamling.

The plan to recruit Local Defence Volunteers in 1940 met with an immediate response all over the country. The name was soon changed to the Home Guard (although they were known affectionately as 'Dad's Army'). By the end of 1940 the Home Guard numbered one-and-a-half million men and during the preparations for D-Day in 1944 they took over most of the security duties on the home front. These men from Brixham played an important part in the Second World War and, after their final muster in 1945, much appreciation was felt by all for the voluntary work they had done during the difficult days of war.

The Primitive Methodist Sunday school children parading in St Mary's Square, *c.* 1929. The Primitive Methodists used to have a meeting house in Milton Street. (Courtesy of Ralph Gardner)

Opposite, above: Uncle Tom's Children's Hour at Brixham Baptist church, *c.* 1945. Brixham children will look back with great affection on the happy Tuesday evenings spent with 'Uncle' Tom Stapleton and 'Auntie' Bessie. Tom is on the left and Bessie on the right.

Opposite, below: A group of happy children at *Uncle Tom's Children's Hour, c.* 1953.

Brixham Rugby Club 1947/48 season. From left to right, back row: Mr Mudge, J. Elliott, E. Caunter, W. Coysh, N. Horsham, R. Dart, J. Caunter, G. Rowe, C. Richardson. Middle row: J. Braddick, S. Edmonds, J. Merchant (capt.), W. Jackson, M. Andrews, W. Foot. Front row: C. Gregory, R. Seaward, R. Gove.

Brixham rugby football team First XV, 1972/73 season, the youngest senior team to play in Devon. From left to right, back row: G. Maddick, J. Dart, M. Dodd, R. Mitchell, G.R. Lovell, R. Gardner, K. Gardner, P. Hayden. Front row: C. Pillar, A. Houcke, T. Brooks, G. Markey, A. Brooks, R. Dart, L. Harvey, P. Harris. (Courtesy of R. Gardner)

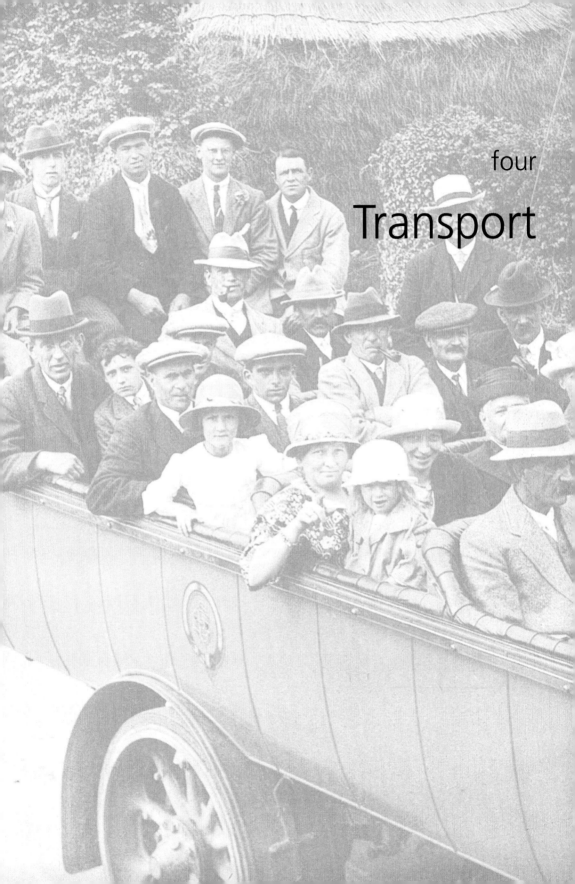

four

Transport

Above: The *Duchess of Devonshire*, Brixham, 1902. The pleasure steamer the *Duchess of Devonshire* conveyed passengers to Bournemouth and Weymouth from Torbay, calling on the way at Sidmouth, Seaton and Lyme Regis. Although these towns had no pier, passengers got ashore via a small bridge thrown out to the beach from the boat. In 1934 the *Duchess* was wrecked at Sidmouth, having got into difficulties because of a heavy swell, and came in on Sidmouth beach broadsides.

Below: Motor launch *Western Lady* leaving Brixham, *c.* 1950. Much loved by day trippers, the *Western Lady* operated in Torbay.

Landing from The "S. S. Pioneer" Brixham. 10043

Above and below: During the heyday of Devon's seaside resorts, holiday makers and trippers who travelled to the coast found many delights to please old and young alike. There was usually something for everyone's taste. Trips along the coast, calling at various ports, became a favourite and in the top photograph, taken in 1907, passengers in full Edwardian finery can be seen landing at Brixham harbour from the SS *Pioneer*. In the bottom photograph the SS *Pioneer*, with a full cargo of passengers, is leaving Brixham around 1905. Brixham trawlers can be seen in the background.

The Blue Anchor Inn on the Quay, *c.* 1955. The driver standing on the right is ready with one of Burton's Coaches to take these people on the annual mens' pub outing. No doubt they had already loaded up a few crates of beer in the boot of the coach, and were all looking forward to a great day out.

Opposite, above and below: After the First World War a revolution took place in transport, with local bus services expanding rapidly. Firms like Burton's and Grey Cars provided motor coaches to visit beauty spots in the West Country. In the top picture we have the Modbury Wesleyan Church Choir outing on a day trip to Brixhain, 9 August 1923. In the bottom picture a Grey Car motor coach, which operated a service from Paignton and Churston to Brixham during the 1920s. The passengers are wearing a variety of hats. I wonder – did they all stay on when the driver got his charabanc up to 20mph, or was it a case of numerous pit stops to retrieve lost headgear?

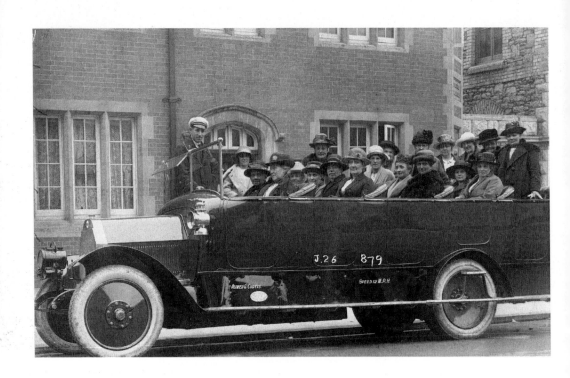

One of Grey Cars' charabancs is pictured here loading passengers outside Brixham Town Hall, *c*. 1928. The occasion is unknown, but the passengers are all boys.

Opposite, above: An Oliver and Curtis charabanc pictured outside the old police station at Bolton Cross, *c*. 1924. This vehicle had a maximum speed of 12mph, and could seat four abreast. One of the most pleasurable features of these trips was the chance to have your picture taken in the photo call.

Opposite, below: One of the most revolutionary changes after the First World War was the coming of the motor bus, which was then known as a charabanc. Here a party are seen in one of Grey Cars' Torpedo coaches, outside the Northcliffe Hotel. In such photographs the hood on the vehicle always seems to be down. Was this to help the photographer, or did the sun always shine then? Perhaps our grandparents were so hardy that they were impervious to the weather.

Above and below: The Victorians may have been the first to declare 'we do like to be beside the seaside', but for many holiday makers the arrival of the charabanc early in the last century brought a new type of holiday – the classic tour, criss-crossing the country and linking resorts. At the vanguard of these new tour operators in Devon was Greenslade's, named after its founder and launched before the First World War. In the top picture we have a fine AEC coach from Greenslade Tours in Bank Lane, with Brixham Bus Station in the background, *c.* 1968, and in the bottom picture is a splendid GUY coach from local firm Burton's, en route to Barry Head, 7 August 1952.

Above: Blackler's General Stores, Middle Street, *c.* 1925. The car parked in the street outside the stores is a Model T Ford. With tongue-in-cheek humour it was said that the Model T could be bought in ten shades of black, or that with 'a piece of tin with a length of cord – join them together and you get a Ford'.

Below: This fine photograph of Brixham station, around 1905, shows the station in all its Edwardian splendour. Brixham was connected with the Dartmouth and Torbay branch of the Great Western Railway by a branch line from Churston station, two miles in length.

Above: The Brixham rail branch line opened in 1868 and pictured here is *Queen*, the first engine used on the line. In the early days, like most lines, the track was broad gauge, but at a later date the rail company recognised that narrow gauge was the way ahead, and the line was changed accordingly. The driver was exposed to all wind and weather, it must have been a cold, wet job in the winter.

Left: A fine picture of the railway engine *Prince* at the fish loading bay at Brixham. The rail link from Brixham to Churston station enabled fish to be sent to London and provincial markets, putting the fishery on a competitive footing with the North Sea ports.

The Brixham branch train waits in the bay platform at Churston, *c.* 1950. The Links Hotel is in the background. The Torbay line extended to the Kingswear terminus in 1864 and the little Brixham branch from Churston opened in 1868.

A single car unit at Brixham railway station, *c.* 1962.

An 0-4-2 Tank Engine No. 4827, 4800 Class is seen at Brixham station with an auto train on 23 August 1945. This engine was built at Swindon by Collett in November 1937, and was re-numbered No. 1427 in November 1946.

Brixham station, 1960. It took seven minutes to run the two miles from Churston to Brixham. Class 1400 engines were used on the branch line – a No. 1466, pictured here, was known locally as the 'Brixham whippet'.

With an absorbing passion for using their cameras on anything and everything, pre-war railway photographers have left behind a rich legacy of pictures. Engine No. 1439 is seen here at Brixham station in the old GWR days. The fireman is leaning out from the cab, and the engine driver, standing outside, is holding an oil can. The other two men were station staff.

This view of Brixham station, with the signal box to the right, was taken in GWR days. Men of the Brixham branch line, staff of the Permanent Way department, can be seen walking up the line.

A 1400 class engine on the Brixham branch line, *c.* 1955. The line closed to passenger service on 13 May 1963 under the Beeching Act. For nearly 100 years passengers used the branch line at Brixham. Excited holiday makers arrived and left, people travelled to and from work, businessmen left for appointments, and men from Brixham went off to war. Year after year the changing pageant swept along the metalled track, until that sad day when a great silence fell upon the line.

This excellent railway picture, full of much detailed information, was taken during the 1940s. It is pictured at Brixham station, shadowed by fish and coal trucks in the background.

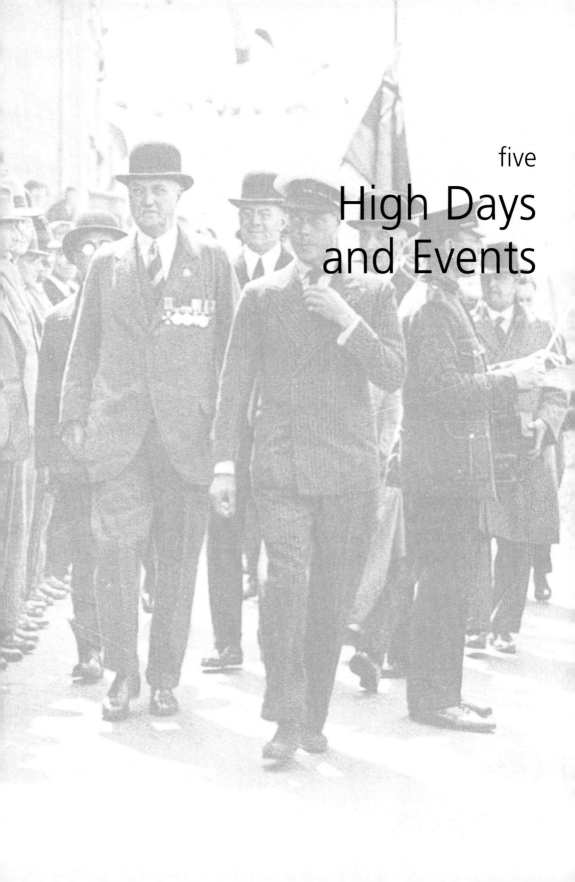

five

High Days
and Events

The coronation of King George V was a day for celebration throughout the country. Every town and village formed a committee to arrange activities for the great day, and everywhere the streets were lavishly decorated. Processions, parties, sports and many other attractions were the order of the day, and the memory of these celebrations stayed with people for the rest of their lives. In this picture, taken on Coronation Day 22 June 1911, the people of Brixham are taking part in a celebration parade.

Opposite, above: Regatta Day, Brixham, *c.* 1905. We catch a glimpse of Edwardian Brixham at leisure in this atmospheric and informative photograph of a crowded scene in a fairground on the Higher Green, Furzeham. There were many delights to please old and young alike, with numerous side shows all vying with one another for attention. The men operating the swing boats on the right, coupled with the stalls in the background, enrich the scene with period flavour.

Opposite, below: A big attraction in Brixham in 1910. Hancock's Fair from Bristol had set up the fairground on the Higher Green, Furzeham, for Regatta Day. Furzeham School is in the background.

In August 1907 twenty boys, led by two men, pitched their tents on Brownsea Island in Dorset. The boys were gathered from all walks of life, and for two weeks they learnt to live in the open and to cultivate comradeship. From this small beginning the Boy Scout movement was born and Baden Powell, their leader, was on his way to becoming a world figure. Scout troops were soon formed in Brixham and here, taken at a date in the 1920s, we have a group photograph of a Scout and Guide gala which took place in the town.

Opposite above: Peace celebrations at Bolton Cross, 11 November 1918. The Great War had ended and throughout Brixham there was a tremendous atmosphere of excitement and elation. However, the joyous celebrations were, for many, a time of sadness – these were the mothers and fathers, the wives and the children who knew that their loved ones would never return.

Opposite, below: Such a sight we will never see again. Hancock's, the fairground people from Bristol, are manoeuvering a Burrell traction engine, No. 1740, around the Overgang hairpin bend. The traction engine is towing the centre truck for the four-abreast set of gallopers (a kind of roundabout).

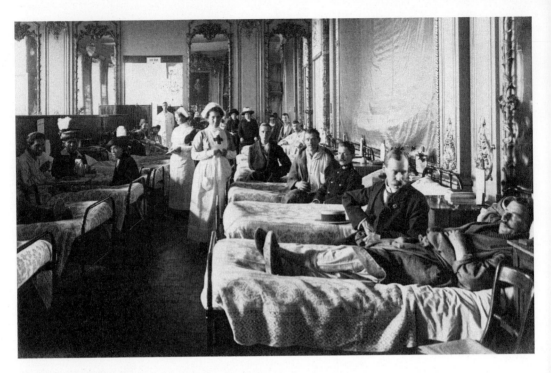

Above: Members of the Voluntary Aid Detachment (VAD) attending to wounded servicemen during the 1914-18 war, in the Cottage Hospital, Cavern Road, Brixham. Although members of the VAD worked entirely voluntarily, they were much involved in the hard reality of wartime nursing, and by the end of the war had proved their usefulness. They were much loved by the convalescing soldiers, who nicknamed these angels with red crosses on their uniforms 'Very Artful Darlings' or 'Victim Always Dies'.

Left: The unveiling of the Cenotaph in Whitehall, by King George V on 12 November 1920, was followed by an impressive countrywide two minutes' silence. War memorials appeared in every village, town and city throughout the country, and here in Brixham in 1922 crowds gather for the dedication of the local war memorial.

Above and below: The Prince of Wales' visit to Brixham, 27 July 1932. Loved for his charm, his humility and his goodwill, the Prince received an ecstatic reception wherever he went. Everyone wanted to get close to him and to touch him, so that by the end of these visits he was often covered with bruises. He was in Brixham for the christening of the lifeboat *The George Shee.* In the top picture the Prince, followed by W.H. Smardon of Brixham and Sir Harold Clayton, can be seen inspecting the lifeboat crew. In the bottom picture, on the same day, he can be seen with that nervous touch to his tie which was characteristic of him inspecting First World War veterans and lifeboat men.

The lifeboat *George Shee* is pictured here just after her launch in July 1932. This lifeboat was named after Sir George Shee, Secretary of the RNLI from 1910 to 1931.

Children gather around on the Top Green, Furzeham, to marvel at two elephants from a visiting circus, around 1935.

Crew members from HMS *Squirrel* are seen here on statue-cleaning duties, giving the William, Prince of Orange statue on the Strand a wash and brush-up.

The death of King George VI was followed on 2 June 1953 by the coronation of Queen Elizabeth II. The people of Brixham once again celebrated with a full day of events. This fish stall on the quay was suitably decorated for the occasion.

Severe flooding affected Brixham during the early part of 1947. Heavy falls of snow froze and lay on the ground for three to four weeks and, following a quick thaw, so much water rushed down the valley that the drains could not cope. Bolton Cross became a lake extending from Parkham Hill up Bolton Street and New Road. Here at Bolton Cross a Devon General half-cab bus can be seen making its way through the floods.

Princess Alexandra is shaking the hand of crew man Ken Thomas after the christening of the new Torbay lifeboat, *The Princess Alexandra of Kent*, 24 July 1958. Also shown are Ken's wife, Joy, Peter Easton and his sister Mrs Burridge. (Courtesy of Ken Thomas)

The charm and warmth of the Queen Mother's manner, coupled with her almost religious dedication to duty, endeared her to the British public, and she received an affectionate and enthusiastic welcome on her many tours. Brixham is no exception, and she is pictured here during her visit to the Brixham Trawler Races, in 1969, and is presenting the Best Kept Trawler award to Harry Thomas. Standing on the right is the Chairman of Torbay Borough Council. (Courtesy of Ken Thomas)

The colourful spectacle of the carnival is very much a part of the Brixham calendar, and the Cowtown Carnival, which was formed to raise money for local charities, has raised and donated many thousands of pounds to deserving causes. The float, with four ladies in big hats and the caption 'COWTOWN HERE US COME BE 'E READY FER US', won the first prize in the Cowtown Carnival of 1971.

MAYFLOWER II. LAUNCHED AT BRIXHAM, 1957

The *Mayflower II*. A replica of the *Mayflower*, the ship in which the Pilgrim Fathers sailed to America, was built in Brixham in 1957. The building began on 4 July 1955 and the shipbuilders chosen for the task were J.W. and A. Upham of Brixham. The architect and design agent was W.A. Baker, and patrons included Admiral of the Fleet Lord Fraser of North Cape GCB, His Grace the Duke of Argyll, Maj. Gen. Sir Francis de Guingand KBE, CB, DSO, Sir Alfred Bossom Bt, MP, J.E. Chapple Esq, Dr H.M. King MP, and Robert Mathew Esq, MP. Shipbuilding had been carried on at Brixham from time immemorial, and it was perhaps fitting that J.W. and A. Upham were asked to build the *Mayflower II*. They had, at that time, been building wooden vessels for more than 150 years and could call on craftsmen with father-to-son reputations for shipbuilding. The *Mayflower II* was 90ft long and 26ft in the beam. One hundred and eighty-three tons, she was barque-rigged and would draw 11ft. The sails were made of flax, and some twelve tons of rope went into her construction. Thirty-five men from Uphams were employed on her, including shipwrights, riggers and carpenters. The keel was laid on 28 July, with a simple civic ceremony and benediction. The story of the *Mayflower II* captured the imagination of the entire country, and after its launch the boat sailed from Plymouth, re-enacting the leaving of the Pilgrim Fathers. Captain Villiers, with his crew of twenty-one and thirty passengers, retraced the historical journey across the Atlantic, sailing into Plymouth, Massachusetts on June 17. The *Mayflower II* found her permanent berth where the Pilgrim Fathers made their home in America.

Above: The *Mayflower II* July 1956, deck construction and planking. The woodwork was slow and difficult because there was not one straight plank in the whole ship

Right: A nineteenth-century advertisement for J.W. and A. Upham, the shipbuilders who built the *Mayflower II.*

J. W. & A. UPHAM
BRIXHAM

P. A. UPHAM, Proprietor

Awarded Silver Medal and Diploma of Honour, 1883

Ship and Boat Builders
CABIN CRUISERS
COMPLETE INSTALLATIONS AND REPAIRS

Spar Makers & Ship-Smiths

Good accommodation for the laying up of small Yachts and Motor Boats for the Winter Months

The *Mayflower II*. Here we have some of the skilled workforce from J.W. and A. Upham fitting shelf to the interior of frames.

The seventeenth-century bell given by Brixham to the *Mayflower II*.

Spectators look with interest at the building of the *Mayflower II*, 1956. The noticeboard on display gives specifications of the boat.

The sea dominates any view of Brixham, and it seems natural that the town was the home of the British Seaman's Orphan Boys for most of the past century. This memorable picture of the boys dressed in their smart sailor suits, with their musical instruments, was taken in 1956. The replica of the *Mayflower* can be seen in the harbour, behind them.

At the Opening of the New Wing (1912), British Seamen's Orphan Home, Berryhead Road, Brixham.

The British Seaman's Orphan Boys' Home in Berry Head Road was first enlarged in 1873, allowing accommodation for fifty boys. In 1890 a new wing was built at a cost of £1,400, and a second new wing was added in 1912. Pictured here are local dignitaries at the opening ceremony.

Dinner, British Seamen's Orphan Home, Berryhead Road, Brixham.

The boys of the British Seaman's Orphan Boys' Home sit to attention in the dining room before their midday meal. Although the room appears to be large, with a high ceiling, the atmosphere in this place is reminiscent of Charles Dickens' *Oliver Twist*.

The Upper School, British Seaman's Orphan Boys' Home, 1912. The British Seaman's Orphan Boys' Home for the Western Counties was established in Berry Head Road in 1859 by William Gibbs of Tyntesfield, near Bristol, for the purpose of making provision for the orphan sons of seamen. A new building near to Rock House was opened in December 1863 and completed in 1864. A new wing was built in 1888 and a second wing in 1912.

The kitchen in the British Seamen's Orphan Boys' Home in Berry Head Road, 1912. The stone-floored kitchen, well-filled dresser and the splendid kitchen range provide an insight into a bygone age.

The boys from the British Seaman's Orphan Boys' Home, Brixham, are seen here ready to take part in a George V coronation procession on 22 June 1911.

The boys of the British Seaman's Orphan Boys' Home are preparing to march off in parade to celebrate the Coronation of King George V, 22 June 1911. The flags and banners they are carrying represent the colonies of the British Empire. For these boys it must have been a memorable day, one to remember for the rest of their lives.

six

Around the Bay

Above and below: These pictures of St Mary's Bay Holiday Camp at Brixham, taken in the 1950s, remind those who knew this period of scenes, places and characters of their youth. In the top picture you can see the line of chalets built to accommodate the holiday maker, evoking the nostalgia of the television series *Hi-De-Hi.* The bottom picture gives a view of the putting green and the games room. St Mary's Bay Holiday Camp provided affordable holidays for the workers to get away from the big cities.

The Shoalstone outdoor bathing pool, 1937.

St Mary's Bay, Brixham, *c.* 1959. St Mary's Beach was a popular venue for locals and holiday makers alike. The low-slung canvas and wooden deckchairs pictured here were essential for anyone who wanted to relax on the beach.

The Battery Gardens arch, looking across to Churston Quay. This public open space was used for defence purposes since the seventeenth century, including the last two world wars.

Chelston, the Old Dairy, 1871. This old dairy was pulled down around 1890. It stood at the junction of Walnut Road and Old Mill Lane, seen here leading up the hill. This was the old road between Torquay and Paignton and is still in use. In views like this the sense of the passage of time is overwhelming and we are reminded of how quickly things change. (Courtesy of the E.S. Gosling collection)

Fishcombe Cove, Brixham, *c.* 1950. This pleasantly cool and sheltered beach, free from westerly winds, has a compelling atmosphere and still remains a popular place for locals and holiday makers alike.

Opposite, above: Oddicombe Beach, *c.* 1890. A day at the seaside has been a distinctive feature of English life since railways made journeys to the sea possible for the majority of people. The rapid development of Torbay resulted in beaches like Oddicombe becoming popular. In 1926 access to this delightful beach was made easier by the opening of the cliff railway, and since that date millions of people have travelled in this way. (Courtesy of the E.S. Gosling collection)

Opposite, below: Fishcombe, Barney and Churston Coves, *c.* 1924. A quiet scene entirely unspoilt and looking very much as it must have done for hundreds of years before. Way back in the smuggling days, these coves were ideal locations to bring in illegal cargo.

Left: Mudstone, Brixham, *c.* 1905. The beach was crowded with what appears to be a Sunday school treat. The church or chapel was then probably the main thing for many people, and the annual school treat, with an excursion to the seaside, was looked upon with huge delight.

Below: The Old Fort and Tea House, Berry Head, *c.* 1914.

Day trippers to the seaside would usually take a picnic with them – indeed, before the 1890s foreshore cafés were unknown. However, by 1908 a tea hut had appeared on Mudstone Beach, and in this picture the staff await to serve holiday makers.

CHURSTON CHURCH near BRIXHAM.

Churston church, *c.* 1920. This fifteenth-century church stands close to Churston Court, an attractive Elizabethan house. The village of Churston Ferrers occupies the narrow neck of land between the south shore of Torbay and the Dart estuary, and looks down from a height towards Brixham.

A fine aerial view of Berry Head, around 1960, showing the Old Guard House café and quarrying operations. The area was noted for its high-quality limestone, formed in shallow seas with coral banks, during the middle upper-Devonian period.

The Beacon lighthouse and coastguard station, *c.* 1920. This lighthouse, which came into service at the beginning of the twentieth century, is both the shortest and highest in the country. Its position on a 200ft-high cliff explains the 'highest' claim, and the shortest is self-explanatory.

Tony Burke, seen here during May 1982, was another of those accomplished artists who were attracted to Brixham by the picturesque qualities of the town. (Courtesy of the *Express and Echo*)

Torre Abbey Sands at high tide, showing the crowds of holidaymakers enjoying the sun in the summer of 1959. (Courtesy of the E.S. Gosling collection)

Right and below: During the early years of the twentieth century, for many people the event of the year was the annual trip to the seaside. It was also the golden age of the postcard. The first seaside postcards to appear bore views of local buildings or beauty spots, and topographical cards have continued to be a staple of the postcard industry to the present day. In the right-hand side postcard we have a view of an old Elizabethan House at Brixham, printed by Valentine's of Dundee in 1907. The one below shows a view named 'on our way to Mudstone', *c.* 1914.

Aerial view of Torquay, 1965. This view extends from Torbay in the foreground, with Peaked Tor on the right, to Babbacome Bay in the background, with Long Quarry point on the right – a distance of 1¾ miles. The museum is in the centre beside the Wesley church with a cleared site behind and Babbacombe Road in front. In the centre is the Imperial Hotel, much enlarged in recent years.

One can't help feeling happy at BRIXHAM

The early days of the twentieth century saw the heyday of the picture postcard, and holidaymakers, who paid an annual visit to the seaside, found a unique genre of postcards to send home. This delightful example was sent from Brixham to Forest Gate, London, in 1919.

The international Protestant organisation, known as The Salvation Army, was founded in 1865 by William Booth and they are known for the good work they carry out in the community to those in need of help and comfort. Pictured here are members of The Brixham Salvation Army band resplendent in uniforms and with their instruments.

Opposite: The coming of peace after the 1914–18 war was a great relief to the people of Brixham, and on 19 July 1919 the whole country joined in a day of peace celebrations. In this picture are the Tribble family of Middle Street, who had gathered together to celebrate.

Left: Southern Quay, 1900, showing the statue to William, Duke of Orange, before the guns were removed.

Below: Officials of the new Torbay lifeboat at Brixham (1927-30). Among those pictured are H.C. Slade (secretary), W.G. Sanders (coxswain), J.W. Gill (District Officer Coastguard), H.M. Smardon (Secretary of Torbay Brixham harbour).

The RNLI was founded in 1824, following an appeal by Sir William Hillary, who lived at Douglas, Isle of Man. Before that date there were some locally run lifeboats around the coast of the British Isles, but there was little co-ordination of effort and it was felt that there was a need for a national service. Since then, Britain's lifeboat crews have been putting to sea to save lives. Their skills and courage, given voluntarily, have resulted in over 120,000 people being saved. Brixham is typical of towns with a lifeboat station where crew join the service, serve varied periods of time, then slip quietly away. Like other lifeboat stations, Brixham is fortunate in that volunteers always come forward to enable a lifeboat to be launched. Here we see the crew who were involved in the rescue of the Dutch barge in 1960. From left to right: Fred Park, Jim Harris, Harry Thomas (coxwain), Peter Easton, John Fry, Ken Thomas, Abe Bartlett, David Thomas, Dick Harris. (Courtesy of Ken Thomas)

Left: This study of a fine old Brixham fisherman was taken on the middle pier before the 1939-40 war. The name of the man is unknown.

Below: These Brixham trawler men proudly display the cups they have won in the regatta. This generation of trawler men were known for good seamanship.

At the southern end of Tor Bay the picturesque harbour and the narrow streets of Brixham are shown here in this fine photograph taken during the summer of 1965. This part of Brixham, grouped about the quay with its tall buildings chock full of windows, gives the town a dramatic beauty not found anywhere else in Devon. (Courtesy of the *Express and Echo*)

Other local titles published by The History Press

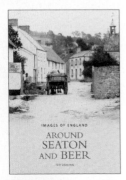

Around Seaton and Beer
TED GOSLING

This collection of over 200 images portrays life in and around the East Devon town of Seaton over the last 100 years. Alongside images of the surrounding villages, this book records the many social gatherings that have taken place in this liveliest part of the Axe Valley. Accompanied by informative captions, this volume will delight all those who have lived and worked in this attractive coastal area.

0 7524 3052 1

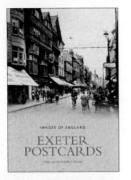

Exeter Postcards
JOHN AND MARGARET FOLKES

This is an exploration of Exeter and Exonians, in the dramatic first six decades of the twentieth century, seen through over 200 archive postcards. Subjects examined include momentous events such as the arrival of the first aeroplanes ever seen by Exonians and the many crises of accidents, fires, floods and war. Exeter Postcards provides a fascinating visual history of the city, which will surprise some and reawaken memories for others.

0 7524 3474 8

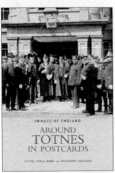

Around Totnes in Postcards
TOTNES IMAGE BANK AND ROSEMARY DENSHAM

This selection of 180 postcards from the Totnes Image Bank collection illustrates the bustling history of this town and the surrounding area, including Dartington, Ipplepen and Ashprington. The ancient castle and Elizabethan buildings are featured and events such as carnivals, Empire Day celebrations and the relocation of the Victoria Memorial Fountain are recalled. The images will evoke memories for some and provide a fascinating glimpse of the past for others.

0 7524 3190 0

Dartmoor
TOM GREEVES

The rich history of Dartmoor can be seen in the 200 archive photographs and postcards in this book. The images recall life as it once was on Dartmoor: the towns, villages and local people who lived and worked on the moor between the 1860s and the 1950s. From farming and mining to social gatherings such as hunts, races and fairs, each picture records the everyday life of these resilient communities.

0 7524 3146 3

If you are interested in purchasing other books published by The History Press, or in case you have difficulty finding any of our books in your local bookshop, you can also place orders directly through our website

www.thehistorypress.co.uk